# A Dog's Love

## Jenna Lee Lethbridge

 FriesenPress

One Printers Way
Altona, MB R0G 0B0
Canada

www.friesenpress.com

Special thanks to Ingrid Rudnik-O'Gorman, my beautiful and talented mother in law who painted the cover of this book. She is an unbelievably talented artist and her work can be found on instagram @dragonflystudioiroart.

ISBN
978-1-03-917551-8 (Hardcover)
978-1-03-917550-1 (Paperback)
978-1-03-917552-5 (eBook)

*1. PETS, DOGS*

Distributed to the trade by The Ingram Book Company

# Table of Contents

# Introduction

**THIS IS THE STORY OF AXEL AND ME:**

When life brings us a dog, the bond is one that cannot be measured or compared. When life brought me Axel, I wasn't well and fumbled along trying to find myself in heartbreak. He helped me heal. Our bond was exactly what I needed at that moment.

A dog's love reaches our souls, and the connection is unlike any other. I write this after Axel crossed the rainbow bridge. I feel empty and whole at the same time. He helped shape me and was there through all my struggles. He was my best friend, and, without him, I feel lost. I cherish our time together and wrote this book to share our adventures. There are others who know this bond and I wish to honour it.

A dog's love is unconditional. It reaches depths that humans will never understand. They are dependable, always there when we need them most, bum shaking, tail wagging, and ready to brighten our day.

I don't believe that some people are not dog people, they simply haven't met the right dog.

I did, and it's better to have love and lost, then never to have loved.

And so, our story begins.

**A Dog's Love:**

My book has been written to honour not only a dog's love, but those who have loved and lost their furry family members. As you read, may you feel comforted in knowing you are not alone in your grief. A dog's love is more than special. At times, they may be your only companion and your only sense of security. In those moments it's hard to imagine life without them.

I wrote this book shortly after saying a final goodbye to Axel after fourteen years together. Writing helped me cope with my grief, as well as celebrate memories. Axel and I had a long journey together filled with ups and downs. We met early in my career as a veterinary technician. Shortly after changing careers to become a nurse, he started to decline, which lead me to the most difficult decision I ever was forced to make.

<u>December 28, 2022</u>

> Today I said goodbye to our family dog after fourteen years. During those moments my heart shattered. It has been the greatest loss I ever have felt. I feel as though one of my children is missing, leaving my heart with a hole.

This is how other pet owners feel after they say goodbye to their beloved furry family pet. I have witnessed it many times. My story addresses the love and relationship we build with our pets. It is about the impact they leave on our lives. It is a love story through and through. Some may read it and say, "But he was just a dog." Others will feel my words as intensely as I do.

Be prepared to cry!

Be prepared to feel all the "feels."

I invite you to share with me how you met your furry loved ones and the impact they left on your life. Follow my Instagram account @adogsloveunited for updates and to share your stories.

Happy reading!

# Chapter 1:
# The Beginning

**IF YOU'VE EVER OWNED A DOG,** you know how special they are. Growing up, I had many dogs, and each left a special pawprint on my heart. I found my love for dogs started at an early age. I found security and comfort in their love. As a child of divorce my life was full of change. Don't get me wrong, I had a wonderful childhood but like any child of divorce, it didn't come without scars.

Our first dog was "Shadow," a German Shepherd puppy, full of spunk, and I remember the day we got her. She stood in our small kitchen mauling me with kisses. I named her after the stuffed dogs from the Nineties whose lips could be lifted to show them snarling. Shadow was the first dog I remember. I was five years old and just starting kindergarten. Funny how our childhood memories stick. Shadow stayed overnight at the veterinary clinic. I missed her like crazy! When she came home, she had to wear a T-shirt to avoid licking her incision area. As a child, I found this hilarious. I remember the smell of the vet clinic when we dropped her off and picked her up. Years later, after earning my veterinary technician diploma, I applied for a job at the same clinic and, oddly enough, the smell was the same. I had flash backs to when we had brought Shadow there. This was a staple in my life and lead me to my early career.

Shadow was my first dog love. She came into my life at a time of tremendous change (my parent's divorce) and gave me the love and security I needed. Unfortunately, time passed, and my mother and I moved. Having to say goodbye added to the anxiety of the change.

This is where it all began. My love for dogs, and their impact on my life. As my first, she will forever be in my heart. It wasn't long after our move (at least in my childhood memory), that I found my next dog love.

Enter Akita.

Akita was particularly special to me. She was my constant in a time of ongoing change that was unsettling for a nine-year old girl. She was a six-month-old Siberian Husky and was beautiful, as well as wild. My mother's relationship at the time had ended, which meant we would be moving. This time, I moved and lived with my father. I had to change schools. This was the first for me, and the transition wasn't easy. A new school meant new friends, but it was the making friends' part where I struggled.

I loved to play sports and every day at recess, I played basketball with the boys. This made me a target for girls to bully. I was going on ten years old and being called cringe-worthy names. It was a hard transition. Not to mention, the state of my home life, which wasn't the best. Akita made it easier. She was always there bum shaking and tail wagging.

It was good living with my father, but the change was difficult, mostly because the woman he was dating was not warmed to the idea. She made it a difficult time for my father and me. Akita came with me. I needed her and I spent hours outside with her since the wicked witch wouldn't let her inside. The poor dog had to be tied outside all day and night, even in bad weather. It makes me sick thinking about it now. She did have cover in the barn but, for the most part, she was outdoors. I grew so angry at her for getting off her lead. Mostly because of the anxiety it put on me. I wanted her to behave, so that we could stay together. She was just a puppy and needed a home with a family who had time to take care of her. Despite my best efforts, I was a kid and didn't know what I was doing.

Akita had the biggest impact on me. She was my security in a bad situation then was rehomed. The day, pain, and the house still haunt me. My father packed Akita and me into the car and off we went. We arrived at the shelter and I cried so loudly that I'm sure they heard me inside. I had a panic attack and hyperventilated. I watched as my father took her out of the car and into the shelter. She pulled towards me, and I reached for her. As I write this, the pain scars my heart even now. At the time, I didn't understand why we were giving her away but, looking back, she deserved a family that would treat her like a queen. I still wonder what happened to her and pray she found her family. That day was my first heartbreak. I cried and screamed for hours, alone again with no security. My next dog love didn't happy for several years.

Enter Ginger, a Boxer cross Mastiff.

Her name was true to her character. She was bonkers, but I loved that goofy girl! I was thirteen when we got Ginger, and I wrestled with her as Boxers love to do. She loved tug-of-war. Sometimes, she would even let me win! She was unaware of her size and sat on laps as though she weighed twenty, rather than ninety pounds.

Ginger came to me at a time when I really needed her, as dog love often does.

Again, my life had changed. I had moved back with my mother, and we'd finally settled into our home, which, I might add was a trailer. I had changed schools again. This time it was Grade 8. I was the new girl again, bullied again. Ginger's love helped. She was always there, bum shaking rope in mouth, and ready to take my mind off all things negative. She was a constant in another time of change, and I loved her for it. Following Grade 8, Ginger and I had to say goodbye. We still were able to visit from time to time, but it's never the same.

My mother had re-married but, thankfully we lived in the same town. I had found my first love in Grade nine and was over the moon about him. High school can be difficult. My experience for the first year was horrible. Again, I was bullied and pushed to the point of breaking. That is when Jake entered my life, the perfect time as always. I felt wild excitement as we climbed into the truck, and my mother drove to the farm where we would be looking at a puppy. My stepfather likely had no idea. It was a day after school, and I'd been wearing my boyfriend's hockey jacket that I forgot to give back. It was spring, the time, when farmers start spraying the fields with manure. The smell is distinctive. It has been said that smell triggers our memory, and manure is hard to forget.

The barn was huge, and there were seven puppies jumping around inside. Floppy-eared German Shepherds being whacky as they could! There was our guy! One ear refusing to stay up. On the ride home, he vomited on my arm and, the smell has stayed in my memory. I told him that it was okay and that we would be home soon. That silly boy tripping over his own feet, had our hearts. We named him Jake, the middle name of my stepfather's grandfather who had recently passed away. I was the only child and a girl. My mother had always wanted a boy, and here was my brother.

Jake slept with me most nights, and I did the late-night bathroom breaks Although he had come from a barn, he was surprisingly easy to house train. A teenage girl's attention span doesn't last long, and Jake soon became my stepfather's dog, following him everywhere. He was his sidekick. Every time my stepfather went to the barn, Jake had to be there. Every time there was a gopher on our property, the poor thing never had a chance. Jake was the first dog we had from puppyhood until his passing. He was a phenomenal pet and set the bar high for all our other dogs. Mind you, he had his quirks, such as chasing lawn mower tires and occasionally running away. He truly was an amazing dog.

Jake passed away peacefully when I was out of college and living on my own. His hips gradually gave out as they often do with German Shepherds, and my parents had to euthanize him. A profoundly sad day. After Jake, they had a few more dogs, but there remains only one that stood out.

Enter Rueger.

He was the handsomest German Shepherd. Not only handsome, but incredibly smart. Rueger came from owners who lived in a small apartment. They loved him dearly but knew he was meant for the farm and, loved being there. As our dogs often did, he became my stepfather's sidekick, always at the barn helping with the chores and making sure the cattle were behaving. Rueger left this world far too early.

There was panic in my mother's voice when she called. My veterinary technician background immediately kicked in, and I drove to their house. Rueger had become bloated, and he was dying. We placed him in my car; sadly he didn't make it to the veterinarian before passing. Rueger had given me a special kind of love, was attentive to my needs, and could always sense when something was off. He was the only one of my parent's dog's that got to meet my children, and that meant a great deal. He even met my Ax man. Although Axel could be a bully sometimes, Rueger never responded with haste, aside from reminding him whose house it was. One specific incident with the boys happened during my oldest son's first birthday. Yes, a dog fight at a one-year-old 's birthday party. Rueger was near the children, and Axel instinctively became protective of his baby, taking on the giant German Shepherd. Rueger immediately pinned him down and, as I screamed, he snarled as if telling Axel who was boss in his territory.

Ruger was an extraordinary dog and will always be in my heart. I'm convinced he and Ax man are in dog heaven running the farmland together. Axel's love was what I needed at a time when I was spiraling. I had lost my job, my relationship and myself.

# Chapter 2:
# The Heartbreak

**THIS STORY LIKE MANY LOVE STORIES,** began and ended with heartbreak.

On a damp July evening, the sky slowly clouded over as the night crept in. I was in my early twenties, having recently moved back home from college and adjusting to working life. My job at the local veterinary clinic where I had completed my high school co-op program, was stressful to say the least. There I was, a brand-new veterinary technician, alone with no mentor to offer me guidance.

One Tuesday evening after work, my entire life plan changed. I was at home, eating Kraft Dinner and waiting for my boyfriend at the time to arrive. Our love story was slightly strange. We had been connected for a long time, even in Grade eight when we dated for a week or two. Flash forward to high school when I dated one of his good friends for several years, and he dated his first love. It wasn't until my second year of college that I felt a sudden whim to call him. He had always been the boy next door or, in reality the boy four concessions over. I called him one night and asked if he wanted to hang out. Things developed from there. We both felt the connection, and it flourished in that first year.

We had the kind of love that was unconditional; at least I did. I was the girl next door, and he was the boy after high school, my first real relationship. I entered the real world, and we started a life together. Or so I thought.

As usual he was running late, likely due to work. I stood in my pajamas by our kitchen window with my bowl of Kraft Dinner. At the sound of his Chevy truck, my heart sparked to life as it always did. The noise was loud and obnoxious. Typical of a young boy, but I loved everything about it.

He pulled into the driveway, and I trotted out, to greet him. He avoided eye contact, and I knew something was up. Then he spoke the four words that made my world spin.

"We need to talk."

I felt the still undigested food rise from my stomach into my throat. He led me to the tiny tree in the front yard. My stepfather was mowing the lawn at the time, and the noise level was high. I can still smell the dewy air and the freshly cut grass. He proceeded to explain the many reasons that the relationship wasn't working. The only thing I could focus on was keeping from crumbling, and I wasn't doing a good job. My knees were weak, my legs felt like jelly. Nausea took over my body. My heart was breaking, and all I could do was stand there, shivering from nerves and the cool air. In the best cliché format, it even started raining. The words rolled off me like the rain. I crossed my arms in a protective way, praying that we could resolve whatever was wrong. In hindsight, the relationship wasn't all my heart made it out to be but in that moment, it was my entire life.

And just like that, it was over. He got into his truck and drove away. While I stood dumbfounded and utterly broken. What was I going to do now? We had our lives planned. I'd done everything right hadn't I? I heard the truck drive down the road and I watched as he became farther and farther away with no brake lights in sight.

I fell hard, just as hard as I had fallen in love.

My legs finally gave up and I fell to my knees in grief. The weight of my heartbreak set in, and I felt alone. My stepfather didn't say anything, probably unsure of what to say to a stepdaughter having a meltdown on the front lawn. My mother said nothing as well, other then "Did you guys just break up?" I shut down and dragged myself to my room where I cried in a panic for an hour.

The aftermath was full of loss. I'll compare it to the scene in "New Moon" where Edward leaves Bella in the woods. She spends months emotions turned off, feeling the weight of the pain hit her at night. I was Bella until I found strength enough to move on with my life.

There was much loss for me within in those couple of months. It started with heartbreak, then I lost my first real job. And all only a week out from my birthday.

I spiraled.

I felt like a failure, and my self-esteem was shot.

My life had always been full of change, and now was a great opportunity to create more. Everywhere I looked was a reminder of the relationship and my failure. It was time to move forward. I wanted to say goodbye to that version of myself. I was made for more, and this small town could never hold me. The relationship ending was my chance to escape. I had been home for only six months and now, moving out on my own for the first time.

The pain still caught up with me at night as buses drove past, and the streetlight shone into my tiny two-bedroom city apartment. We had been best friends, and I think that is what hurt the most. For nearly a year after the breakup, we hung out on occasion, but it hurt too much, and so we stopped talking all-together. After that, each night became easier. However, I never fully recovered. Every relationship thereafter fell short in comparison to the deep connection and unconditional love I had felt.

That is, until I met him. His big brown eyes stared directly at me. The moment our eyes met I knew this was it. But I wasn't going into this relationship lightly.

Not this time.

# Chapter 3:
# It Was Love at First Sight

**LET ME PAINT THE PICTURE OF** how Axel and I met.

I was fresh out of college and working at a pig barn after being let go from my veterinary technician job. It was a toxic environment with no support or mentorship. I'd graduated from St. Clair College and spent two years in Windsor, Ontario, making lifelong friends. I chose this career for my love of animals and science, but as many do in the profession, I changed careers after eight years.

Being a veterinary technician was not without heart-break. We helped countless families say goodbye to their furry family members. It was heart-wrenching to watch, but it came from a place of love. I never understood how difficult that decision was to make until I stepped into their shoes with my dog of fourteen years.

I had been working at a pig barn in our rural town. My post-college experiences were nothing if not tough. I had gone though considerable loss within a short period of time.

My relationship ended, I'd lost my first job, then, to top it off, I failed my registry examination, which, essentially is the licensing for a career. I felt that I was failing at life, caught in the transition from teenager to adult. I had never failed at anything and had been an overachiever. There was nothing left to do but stop feeling sorry for myself and rise, and that's exactly what I did. Everything in my small town reminded me of the relationship that had ended and of all my other failures. I had to get out as soon as possible. As the new year arrived, so did my new life. I moved into the city for the first time, a country girl with big dreams.

When I moved, I had been working in the pig barn and driving an hour each day. I finally found another job working as an animal control officer at the Humane Society. The job was okay at times, but also hellish. Try to imagine riding in a van with a dead skunk in the dead heat of summer. Or scraping roadkill off a road filled with maggots. I worked part time with the Humane Society and full time at the pig barn. My social life was non-existent, as I didn't have time or the energy to be social. Not to mention that neither jobs were ideal for the dating scene.

Working at the Humane Society filled the nurturing side of me. I saw many animals come and go. There were pets that pulled at my heart strings, but I was used to this and knew the responsibility that owning a pet entailed.

At eleven o'clock one night, as my afternoon shift ended, I received a phone call, "what now?" I'd been on call all night after my shift, not a great job for people who liked to sleep.

The woman had explained that her dog had run away, she was checking to see if he had made his way to the shelter. At shift change, nothing had been communicated about a dog being taken in, but I took her information. My intuition prompted me to physically check. I can still see the look on his face. There he was, his eyes full of questions and an expression that said, "Give me food!"

My heart melted.

It was love at first sight.

I called the woman back to let her know he was at the shelter and tell her about the fee for dogs at large. As expected, she wasn't happy. A week passed and he hadn't been picked up. At this point, animals are entered into the system. The moment he was put up for adoption, I put my name into the mix and made sure to plan my finances for the necessities as well as for walking times and where he would sleep. I even bought a crate. This wasn't a decision I took lightly. I began part-time work at a veterinary hospital in Waterloo, working twelve-hour shifts, which meant he would come with me to the clinic each day. This time, I wasn't wearing rose-coloured glasses but, prepared for a happy relationship without the heart-break.

I couldn't handle the heart break again, still I made the decision to love.

Paperwork was completed and Axel came home with me. His name at the shelter had been "Cheeko," and I still laugh about it. I wanted to give him a more "manly" name and went with "Axel". But, "Cheeko" had suited him well; he thought he was a tiny lap dog.

The night I brought Axel home, I felt nervous but excited. I wasn't sure how he would adjust to my busy schedule but mostly concerned about how much sleep I would get. Despite my nervousness, I was still excited about bringing him home and showing him unconditional love. Shelter life isn't ideal for any dog. It can be very loud and often a scary place for our furry friends (although staff members cuddle the pets as often as they can to help make their stay more tolerable). Despite fears, our first night together was a success. Axel was happy to be out of the shelter. He was a good dog and rarely barked, which had been my primary fear living in an apartment building. We went on daily walks together and enjoyed runs through the park.

In those early days, Axel and I got acquainted with each other and fell into a routine. He came to work with me and, on my days off, we took long walks to release his energy. Some days we spent on the couch cuddling. My roommate at the time was a fellow vet tech I had met in college. She loved Axel as much as I did, and we had a full fur family in that tiny apartment with her two cats, Axel, a snake, and a chameleon. Typical of a vet tech's home.

Our family was just getting started.

Never did I think about life without Axel and how hard it would be.

# Chapter 4:
# Expect the Unexpected

**IN THE BEGINNING,** I saw Axel's imperfections, and he saw mine. I didn't have much patience and, despite my professional background, I felt lost and unsure of what I was doing. Axel was a rescue dog with his own set of issues. Little did I know how much we would help each other.

He was labelled a lab, hound, mastiff cross, but he looked like a bully breed. Bully breeds are not good on leash walks, mainly because they lead with their heads. They also don't always get along with other dogs. This made our leash walks difficult. On multiple occasions, he ran away and left me panic-stricken, calling his name.

During those early days, when Axel and I were getting to know each other, his manners were not very good, and I enrolled him in training classes. An old dog can indeed learn new tricks. A weekly class was offered at the local PetSmart. There I discovered Axel's intense love for caged animals. He would go nuts over a rabbit, and I had to drag him into another aisle to avoid knocking cages over. Only mildly embarrassing.

Not having been socialized, he also showed leash aggression. Over the course of the years, I tried to break this bad habit for him. However, when he was bound and determined to meet the other dog it would often lead to a fight. Instead, I began avoiding other dogs all together. With Axel looking like a bully-breed, I wasn't taking the risk.

As a new pet owner, I made an appointment for Axel to have his post-shelter check up at the clinic where I worked. I had adopted him in June, which meant he was due for his spring examination. Typically, this includes testing for heartworm, and I anticipated his health would be in tip-top shape. Little did I know, Axel and I had more in common then I had thought.

Heartworm wasn't something we saw often. A co-worker called to me as I was cleaning the examination rooms. When I saw the result, I looked at it as if it were a pregnancy test telling me I was going to be a mother. Instead, it told me that the dog I was falling in love with was very sick and might die. My heart sank, and I cried. What would we do now?

As at other times, when life sent me lemons, I found a way to make lemonade.

Heartworm is a parasite transmitted by mosquito bites. The mosquito will carry the tiny heartworm, and when they bite the dog's skin, it enters the bloodstream where it matures and migrates to the heart. Like any parasite, it reproduces rapidly causing inflammation as the heart becomes stressed. Symptoms of heartworm include signs of congestive heart failure, that is what it leads to if untreated or undiagnosed. I'm grateful we found it early since heart damage can be permanent and, thankfully, for Axel it wasn't. We were at a stand-still, Axel's heart was physically threatened and mine was emotionally torn.

Two souls destined to find each other.

Our healing began.

Axel's treatment wasn't easy on him by any means. Heartworm is treated with a drug called Ivermectin, along with heart medication and parasite control. He needed two injections of this medication every two months. Bloodwork was needed as well, and the injections knocked the wind out of him every time. Treatment wasn't inexpensive, and, continued for six months. One year passed before he went into remission. At long last, he was heartworm-free.

Shortly afterward, we were ready for a change. Two hearts had healed and were ready to start life again. I found another Veterinary Technician job in Niagara that aligned with our desired new beginning. The job was Monday to Friday without on-call or weekend duties. It was the break we both needed with the chance to do things on our own. We packed my red Ford Ranger and took to the highway. We would start over again, with full hearts.

As we pulled up to our new home, we took in the scenery and smells. Axel jumped out of the truck whole heartedly taking it all in. He ran around the yard then darted into the apartment after investigating and securing the parameter.

We were home.

The rest of our journey was much the same. We did experience a few bumps that threw us off track, but it wasn't until the devastating news of Axel's diagnosis that life really took an unexpected turn. At the time I shrugged off the vague signs and went about our hectic life. Our family had grown, and our life was in constant chaos. We started in that small apartment just Axel and I; then, over the years our family grew. We were a family of six before having to say goodbye to a be-loved member.

I took it the hardest. Life had begun again with Axel, and I expected he would always be there.

# Chapter 5:
# The Story Begins

**AXEL AND I LIVED** in a quaint town called Queenston, Ontario. It was my first time living alone. just Axel and I in a cute apartment in a house. Queenston, is a beautiful town I'd highly recommend visiting.

In my tiny apartment I experienced my first family loss. It had been a perfect day in March, I'd biked to work and still can feel the mild breeze on my cheeks and see the sun rise over the trees. The day is forever imprinted in my mind. It was such a beautiful day in March. As I listened to my music while pedalling, I felt free and full of life. Little did I know that someone I loved was slowly leaving the earth. I took in the surrounding beauty as my grandfather faded away.

My family had tried to contact me all day, but I had left my cellphone at home. When I returned, there was a message from my mother on my landline. I knew something was wrong as I returned her call. The news that my grandfather had passed away left me heart-broken and distraught. I was five hours away, living alone in a town new to me. But I wasn't alone; Axel was there holding me up when I wanted to fall over. He was there licking my tears, listening to my sobs of regret at not going to see my grandfather earlier. As my one true friend, he has seen me through every heartache, helping me put the pieces back together. He taught me unconditional love.

It took a long time to get over the first major loss within my family but, like any loss, it brought us closer together. A couple of months after my grandfather's passing, my grandmother, Irene was diagnosed with Alzheimer's Disease. My aunt and my father kept telling me of their concern, but I waved it off.

"Oh, that's just Nanny."

"She's always forgetting things."

"Oh, she's just sad Poppa's gone."

On a visit, during a walk with my grandmother and Axel, I witnessed the Alzheimer's Disease for the first time. She had lived in the same house through all my twenty years of life at the time and had forgotten how to get home. The last Christmas my grandmother and I celebrated I had brought Axel. It was the last time I saw her in her home, and I took a photo of her with Axel sitting together on the couch. It was more like hugging. Axel had leaned into her, and she had her arms wrapped around him, both on the couch that I knew so well. That itchy-fabric couch where she and I had spent nights watching "Poppa's" television shows then pulling out the bed for my sleep-overs. Those memories remain dear to my heart. She was the reason I went back to school to become a nurse. I wanted to understand the disease. In time, I was better able to communicate with my grandmother. She had lost her voice and her mobility. I spoke with her often and even once brought Axel into the nursing home to greet her for the last time. She passed away shortly after I learned I was pregnant with Iris, my third child.

Shortly after my grandfather's passing, I faced another loss. As Axel and I adjusted to our new town and apartment, I was let go from my job after six months. They did, however keep me on for another month to let me get things in order. Another loss, another failure. Axel and I did a lot of snuggling during this time. One more loss that Axel was there for, offering me unconditional love while I cried into his fur.

I was let go because I didn't have enough experience, or so they said. This was true, and something they knew when they hired me. It was a huge blow to my self-esteem. The company hired the co-op student as my replacement, and I assumed they had hired me if only to cover while she finished school and while the other technician was off. It was all part of our journey, and so I learned from the experience, picked myself up, and moved on.

In the moment, I think I was upset because I had paid a lot for my expenses and wasn't sure how I would survive. I applied to other clinics but received no replies. Then I did what any responsible person would do and took another job outside of my chosen career. I had to pay bills and I began working at a fast-food restaurant, though it was more of a takeout section of a privately owned restaurant. The people there were kind, supportive, and so much fun! Unfortunately, the wage didn't cover my expenses while living on my own, so Axel and I packed up and moved again.

This time we moved into my boyfriend's mother's house. Not the most ideal situation for a twenty-year old, but a girls got to do what a girl's got to do. It was a struggle after having lived on my own, not to mention this was my first time moving in with a boyfriend. What made it easier was having Axel with me. He was an important part of me, and when he was welcomed with open arms, the transition became that much easier. Axel loved it there. He had reign of the house and beds. My boyfriend's family loved him and gave him lots of snuggles! Most important, my boyfriend adored him. He was living the high life.

It was after a couple of months that I sank into a depression, feeling stuck, trapped even. All I wanted to do was sleep. I worked periodically at the restaurant, usually late shifts. I had little to no social life and, I felt like a failure again. All my friends excelled in their vet tech careers, while I worked far removed from my career and lived in my boyfriend's mother's house. He was very supportive, making the time easy, but even he couldn't fix the way I felt. Again, I felt broken, facing another failure.

As at other times I felt stuck, I looked for a desperately needed change. I had to pull myself out of a slump. Axel helped, making life both exciting and frustrating at times, but he distracted me in the best ways. One morning, he was hesitant to eat his breakfast, which I thought was odd. Later, I discovered he had eaten the entire pizza I brought home from work the night before along with half the box. Axel loved pizza! Our dog's peculiarities can often distract us from our struggles. Their devotion and quirks make us love them even more, and it was those things that brought us closer together.

With the need for change, I began searching for vet-tech jobs in different area codes. That's when I came across a clinic where I could grow and my career would flourish, and so I applied. My search lead me to the small northern town of Bracebridge, Ontario. The day of my first interview came with a snowstorm in Bracebridge, while in Niagara, there was little snow since it's further south. The interview was cancelled that day, but when we were able to travel up north to discuss the job, I was in awe of the clinic. The staff was wonderful, and it was the ideal place to grow and build my professional confidence. They welcomed Axel and me enthusiastically. Luckily, he was always a willing traveller. This time we were off to Bracebridge in the Muskoka District. I packed up my Ranger and headed to our new home, a comfortable basement apartment in the country where he could run, and we could hike. The landlord had a dog that Axel loved to rough house with. Life was good.

About a year in, things changed, no thanks to my own doing. I was in my early twenties and not ready to settle down. I began going out more and more, to find myself in all the wrong places. It was a time in my life when I had the most fun, but one that pains me to think about. Another relationship ended, and Axel and I were on our own again.

As always Axel was there tail wagging, ready to pick up the pieces. I was packing again. Moving and changing our life again. This would be the time when we met our forever person and the home where everything started to change for us.

I found a pretty townhouse room to rent. My roommate had two husky dogs, one of which Axel didn't get along with, as he was dominant and so was Axel. Axel spent most of his time in my room rolling around on my bed. On some days, he went to work with me. We lived in town down the road from a beautiful park and water dam, so it made for picturesque runs and walks.

The adjustment was big for us both. I was again transitioning to being on my own, but I wasn't alone because Axman was always there, tail-wagging, forgiving, and ready to give me all the doggy love I could handle. He never judged and simply listened.

After dusting myself off, I decided to distract myself with a date. Ironically it was a boy who had pursued me from work. He was a co-worker's brother. I know right, off limits, but heck I didn't care. I needed to distract myself at the time. I can remember when I opened the door, not really caring until I saw his face and thought he was cute. I answered the door with just blow-dried hair, it was like medusa no lies. He probably thought I was crazy, but he still came in. He brought wine, I was in love already. I set him up with wine glasses and TV in my room, as I finished getting ready. I put my face together and bam, was ready to go. I remember watching Axel's reaction to this new boy in our life, and I watched closely to the new boy's reaction to Axel. It's kind of like introducing your new beau to your kids, you want them to get along.

I distracted myself with a date. Ironically, the boy was a co-worker's brother. I know off limits, but I didn't care. I needed the distraction and though he was cute. I greeted him with just blown-dried hair. I looked like medusa with a head full of snakes. He brought thought I was crazy, but he came in. He'd brought wine, and I was already in love. I set him up in my room with wine glasses and TV as I finished getting ready. I watched Axel's reaction to this new boy in our life, and closely watched the new boy's reaction to Axel. This was like introducing your new beau to your children; you want them to get along.

They got on well, so off we went! Around that time, I travelled to Florida to capture and release manatees for research purposes. The new boy stayed at my place, minding Axel while I was away. The night before I left, Axel and my roommate's dog got into a fight that left Axel with a sore under his eye and placed on eye medications. The new boy, having a vet-tech for a sister, was well versed in medications. I left and, when I returned, the boys had bonded.

It was only a couple of dates later, and within the span of a couple of months, that we were living together in an apartment. Axel loved life! He had his own futon and a place to wander around in. Way better then being cooped up all day in a room. We became a family, adding one more member.

# Chapter 6:
# And Then There Were Three

BY NOW, AXEL HAD BECOME well adjusted to change, as I had throughout my childhood. Change isn't always a bad thing. We were packed, ready to move on to our next adventure: new boy, new apartment, new town. A beautiful apartment above a naturopathic clinic. There was a park down the road with trails where Axel and I could go for runs and walks. It was very modern and a little out of our price range, but well worth the extra money.

On entering there was the living room and, to the left, two bedrooms, one for Axel and his futon. To the right, was our kitchen, which was open to the living room with an enclosed breakfast bar. Everything about the apartment was wonderful, but my favourite part was the deck. With the business below, the owners had built a privacy fence so we couldn't see the road. It was our oasis, and we spent a lot of time there. Axel loved the sun, even when heavily panting he never moved into the shade. He loved the outdoors but had no street smarts. He was curious by nature, and the hound in him always had his nose leading first.

It was at this apartment that Axel made his way over the barricade and down the stairs of our deck. I'd been inside and had left him to his suntanning. When I returned, he was gone. I yelled at the boyfriend of the time, insisting that he should have been watching Axel, although it was as much of my fault as his. This wasn't the first time Axel was missing. He had run away several times, the first being in Queenston when he took off after being off leash in our backyard. The second time was at my parent's farm, where I was sure I had forever lost him to the fields. When I came close to giving up hope, I spotted him in a neighbour's driveway.

This time was much like that. I took to the streets and checked all the most familiar areas around town. But here, instead I ran screaming his name feeling the lump sinking deep in my throat and tears beginning to well. I was about to collapse when I heard it over the street sounds, even over the sound of my frantic heart beating in my ears. The pitter-patter of paws. The way his collar clicked every time he ran. I swung around towards the noise and dropped to my knees, overwhelmed with emotion. Furious yet relieved. I was mauled with his kisses and wagging tail. I gave him a stern talking to, and he promised he wouldn't do it again, but you already know he would! He loved adventure, and well this was only the beginning of ours.

Axel and I had been alone only for a month or so and here we were starting a relationship all over again. With every relationship, the early stages can be rocky, and ours had its fair share of rocks. My boyfriend and I were both young and new to living together. We were still learning about each other, and that can be a hard track to navigate. After our bumpy start, we took to the canoe and challenged our relationship with a back-country camping trip. This was unlike anything I had ever done before.

We drove to a lake, put our stuff into the canoe and rowed until we found a campsite that suited our liking. Axel, a dog with no street smarts, came with us. Try to imagine me, a brown-haired, medium-size woman of five feet, four-inches, my boyfriend, a dark-haired, medium-built man of five feet, nine-inches, two bags of gear and Axel, a sixty-pound bouncy Lab-hound riding between us. Surprisingly he adjusted well to our new travel method, curling up and watching as the water drifted past. He would, occasionally, catch a scent, get excited, and we'd remind him to lie down. Neither of us wanted to end up in the lake with soaking wet gear for the weekend. We canoed to our campsite with Axel perched in the middle, like a lady being courted. This trip was the beginning of another adventure because it opened both Axel's and my eyes to nature and the possibilities. It also was one of the stepping-stones of my relationship. A camping trip means hard work, hot sun, and not a lot of food. It tests us in a good way. Want to build your connection? Go back-country camping; it will make or break you. For Axel and I, it made us. Axel was in his happy place, and so was I. He lay on the rock soaking up the sun, and I sat on the rock fishing all day. It was heaven.

This was the start of our new adventure. We made many back-country trips after this one, and Axel always came with us. We began to see that his soul was born for the wild; hence his lack of street smarts. One of our trips to an island in North Tea, Axel, much to my surprise, camouflaged himself in the bushes and took a nap. It was unlike anything I had ever seen. This island was one we frequented. It is where my now husband, then my boyfriend, became my fiancé. Axel was there, sharing in the photos and fun, not to mention shock.

We spent our last back-country camping trip there, taking out a canoe when I was six months pregnant with our first-born. Axel was there, snuggling into my bump to keep me warm and comfortable. Never could I imagine how sad these camping trips would be without him. He was always there, as excited as I was for our new adventures. The island will forever have significance for us and carry our memories. The little apartment over the naturopathic clinic held a lot of firsts for too. Not only did we take a step towards marriage, but we also added a new furry family member to the mix.

Enter Merc, a medium short haired orange tabby who stole Axel's heart. Not at first, but with time, and these two became inseparable. A dog's love doesn't only benefit humans, but also their furry kin. Merc had been living in the shelter and had tried to bite off his arm after getting it caught in the cage door. The poor cat had lost all feeling in the arm, and I decided to foster, then later, adopt him.

When I brought Mercury home, Axel wasn't a fan. This was his house, and he liked it that way. Merc, on the other hand, was thrilled, never having had a brother before. He immediately went up to Axel and began head-butting him. Thinking back, it could have been the pain medication that left him feeling so good, but they bonded. As cats often do, he became the boss of the house, and Axel simply complied, although I think he secretly loved it. Merc would often snuggle beside him on the bed. They were best friends but, as big brothers do, Axel often was annoyed enough to get up and move. At one point, the boys had been snuggling, then when I looked over again, Axel had left. He'd moved to the couch and was curled into the tiniest ball on Merc's bed.

During Axel's last day on Earth, Merc went to him and snuggled in, something he hadn't done in awhile, as Axel hadn't been feeling well. It was as if Merc were saying goodbye. It was sweet yet heart-breaking to watch.

Axel had been there for me, sharing in every change I'd encountered. Through every struggle and exciting moment. My wedding day was one of those times. I felt immense anxiety that day and had woken in panic. Marriage meant forever. Was this what I wanted? Was this who I wanted to be with?

There was Axel, lying on the end of my bed listening to me and giving me his unconditional love and understanding. He looked at me without judgement and took it in. He kissed my face as it to say it would all be okay.

A dog's love shows no limitations or restrictions but only understanding and compassion. They don't care where we've been but, only that we come home. They don't care about our reactions; they care only that we're all right. They are a piece of who we are. We find each other at a time of struggle and, together, we heal. Leaning on one another in times of hardship, as well as laughing and smiling in times of joy. Life is too hard sometimes, and we need a special someone to help get through. Axel was that special someone for me. He was there every time I needed him.

For that, I will forever be grateful.

# Chapter 7:
# The Years Fly By

**FIRST COMES LOVE, THEN COMES MARRIAGE,** then comes baby in a baby carriage.

It seems surreal looking back to how our journey began and where it ended. Axel's snout had begun to sprout gray hairs. I remember when I'd started to sprout gray hairs, shortly after having children. We had started as two young broken hearts and, merely eight years later, I was a mom and Axel a big brother.

My first pregnancy was special. My husband and I lived in a tiny basement apartment in the country. We had moved there shortly after our engagement to save money for our wedding. It was a big adjustment for us all, but the large yard made up for the space we lacked. It was in that tiny apartment I began feeling strange. I had no idea what pregnancy felt like but, some-how I knew I was pregnant. Axel must have known as well because he was so protective of me and extra clingy during this time. My suspicion soon proved true; I was going to be a mom. And only three months after the wedding. I broke the news to Axel. He had been my only baby for so long, and now he had to share. He wasn't overly impressed, but he knew he had a duty to protect and comfort. Throughout my entire pregnancy he stayed close to me.

There was no way we could have remained in our tiny apartment and raised a baby. The hallway was full of our stuff, and there was no space to walk let alone crawl. My life motto has been, "I'll figure it out," and that's exactly what I did. I found an option that led to buying our first home, and I was six months pregnant when we moved in. It was extremely exciting! Another move and change of scenery. Axel adjusted well, as he always did. He even made friends with our neighbours.

The house was a fixer-upper, but then aren't all first homes? It was a bungalow in the country. The backyard was filled with a garden, as was the front. Our neighbours were kind and often plowed our driveway or cut our grass. We welcomed their kindness especially because, I was far into pregnancy and my husband often worked late. Axel loved this house, our first true home together as a family. We lived close to a farm that Axel and I frequently walked past. Soon, though, our walks became slower and slower. Axel understood, as always, and adjusted to my needs, as I did for him. We spent a lot of time travelling to visit family. As my due date approached, we all grew nervous but excited. We weren't sure what to expect but knew it would be a love like no other.

And for Axel, it was.

One fateful night, ironically the night before our first wedding anniversary, I went into the bedroom and, as I spoke to my unborn child, reassuring him that I was ready, my water broke. There was fluid all over my bedroom floor. I called for my husband, but he ignored me until I screamed at him. Axel was sleeping on his bed in the living room, undisturbed from my distraught calls. My labour quickly progressed to contractions every two or three minutes. I had preplanned a natural birth and now was on all fours, breathing heavily and stating that I would be getting an epidural. I kissed Axel goodbye and let him know that soon our bundle of joy would arrive. Fifteen hours later, we met our first-born son, Henry Franklin Douglas. It was the most beautiful day of my life.

It had been a very long night, and we were exhausted. When we got home, we were greeted by family. My sister-in-law and her husband were there, along with my in-laws. The one greeting us most excitedly was Axel. Bum shaking, and tail wagging, thrilled to meet his brother. I have tears in my eyes as I write. Until now, I had surpassed this memory. It was one that is imprinted on my heart. Much the same as my oldest meeting his little brother for the first time.

Axel was so excited. He gently sniffed Henry in his car-seat and gave him whisker kisses. My husband took Henry out and lowered him down for Axel to meet face to face. I know Axel fell in love. I could feel it. As I bent down, in pain from childbirth, Axel leaned on me and gave me his unconditional love as he kissed my face, like he was telling me, "Good job, Momma!" I can still feel him leaning into me. Never did I realize how much I would miss such a feeling.

The first couple of months as a mother were a hard adjustment. I was still in nursing school while on maternity leave, so I was very busy. When I finally got my bearings, Axel, Henry, and I took many walks. I felt bad for Axel in the beginning since he was limited to these walks. But he didn't mind and was always patient with me, even when I wasn't with him. That's a dog's love, always understanding and never judging.

Shortly after my son's first birthday, my husband and I made plans to take a trip together. A repeat honeymoon after the first child is always needed! After every new family addition, I think a mother and father have more then enough reason for a vacation. I was hesitant to leave and felt a lot of anxiety. It wasn't just leaving Henry, but Axel too. He and I went everywhere together.

It was after we got back that I realized Axel felt the same anxiety. While we were away, my mother and father-in-law took turns watching Axel and Henry. We were gone only one week, but it felt like eternity. While we were away, Axel had shown separation-anxiety behaviours such as peeing in our bed. This behaviour became a significant issue, causing many other issues to arise. For one, Axel's anxiety caused him to become destructive. This increased my anxiety, and I'm sure my reactions intensified his. Looking back, I wish I had handled it with more grace and patience, but I was a working mom who was also going to school part-time. I had neither patience, nor time.

At this time, Axel started to age. I looked at him one day and I saw his gray snout. People would ask me how old Axel was, and I would always reply with the same number, even years later. I was in denial. With Axel's new behaviours, there was no way we could go to work without the house being destroyed. We had to resort to chemical restraint, aka medications. Axel started with Prozac and, although it worked, he slowly began to decline. He took his medication and headed to work my husband, a happy option for us, and he loved it. My husband built houses, which meant he worked outdoors. Axel spent his day sunbathing and was exhausted by the time he came home. He spent an entire summer as a carpenter dog. My husband's coworkers adored him and gave him lots of love and treats on the job. We were able to wean him off the medication, but he had already slowed down.

Our next adventure brought us to my second pregnancy and a son. A growing family means more responsibilities, which meant our time together was less. We still went for walks, but everything became harder. It was after my second child that Axel showed his anxiety again. When Cam had the hiccups as a newborn, Axel for whatever reason would go crazy. He got up and paced as if the hiccups were thunderclouds crashing over our house. It was very strange but something we learned to deal with. It became so bad that Axel would have to sleep at the other end of the house. Shortly after Cam's birth, we decided to move again. We had put our house up for sale and were moving three hours away to the farmland. We were excited, but it was a big adjustment. Again, we packed up our lives and moved. Axel, Cam, Henry, and I all jammed into my overly stuffed VW Tiguan. My husband had the truck packed and ready. We were off onto our new adventure in a new home. Leaving our house was sad, but we left with many good memories, and we were eager to see where new memories would be made.

We moved into my grandparent's rental home where we stayed until we could find our forever home. It was a large, stone, century home, two stories high and creaky at night. The house sat on a hill that faced sunrise and sunset. Each morning, we were greeted with sunshine in our rooms, and we could watch the sun set over the barn. Axel loved being off leash in the fields, and, of course, he loved the cows. He was so good with cattle, and they loved him.

It was in this home I was able to slow down and saw Axel slowing down too. My second son was around six months old, and I was getting my bearings. We had faced so much change and been so busy that I didn't notice Axel's decline. I watched him running in the fields, but it was more a quick burst of energy followed by a slow walk back to the house. It broke my heart. His coordination was off and sometimes his knuckles dragged. I wrote it off as being tired and, I often felt the same exhaustion being a mom. There was no time or energy to emotionally cope. I was in the process of planning my return to work, finding daycare, along with our forever home.

After giving up hope, we found it, and packed our bags one more time. This was the house for us. Axel had his own room in the mud room, where he felt comfortable. But his anxiety worsened as the children grew and, frankly so did mine. The house was never quiet with kids running around, and this made him anxious, which made me anxious. We brought his bed down to the basement to give him a break, and he enjoyed it there. He greeted us when we left and when we came home.

A year after feeling settled, at long last, we learned our life would be changing again. The Covid pandemic had struck, and I had been working in the local hospital when I found out I was pregnant. The news was overwhelming but exciting. Axel was excited too, although he had slowed down much more, he still got up to give me and my bump all his love. Around this time, I had taken him to the local veterinarian for his annual wellness examination and was given his diagnosis. Despite my previous experience, I had never heard of it. What made my heart sink were the words "progressive disease." Axel was diagnosed with degenerative myelopathy. The loss of coordination and knuckling I had noticed at the farm had been the start of the disease.

As time passed, he stopped getting up to greet me when I arrived home. He stopped bum shaking and tail wagging. He wasn't happy, and a piece of me knew it but I chose ignorance to avoid pain. My heart held on, and so did Axel. A busy life had taken me away for awhile but, as I came back, I saw the change. He was suffering and there was only one thing I could do for him. The progression did finally take me to that difficult decision, the one that cripples you. It's done out of love, but that never makes it easier.

# Chapter 8:
# The Decision

**THE DECISION TO EUTHANIZE MY DOG** was the worst decision of my life. Yes, euthanasia can be a merciful thing because it can end suffering, but it is torture for the person making the decision. It is hard to see a long-loved dog suffer and harder to imagine a world without him. The decision to euthanize is a selfless act, and I'm glad I made it but, in honesty, I wavered. I had made the appointment twice, as I couldn't decide on the best time. Our veterinarian and her staff were exceptionally kind and talked me through it. Axel needed a lot of care, and I felt burned out. I was preparing to go back to work, opening a home childcare service, as well as returning to nursing, preparing our home, myself, and our children. I thought about the decision day and night. It was an inside battle with myself. Logic over emotion. I went into full-on hyperventilation mode each night, sitting with Axel and crying into his fur. I kept asking him to tell me when he was ready. Thinking about a final goodbye had me feeling like I was losing the love of my life all over again. I felt lost and alone.

Ultimately, I did the hard thing and booked the appointment. Axel let me know that it was time. He had started to lose bowel control, and I could see the shame in his eyes. It wasn't his fault, and I didn't want him to feel bad. This was a terribly difficult time for both of us. He wanted to hold on for me, and I wanted to be strong for him.

The decision was excruciating, but it had to be done. Thinking about it now, I can still feel the pain all over again. It's almost seven months since I said goodbye, but it may as well have been yesterday. The only difference is that I can accept it now, knowing I made the right decision. We loved one another unconditionally. Sometimes that means letting go though it's the last thing we want to do. It's selfless. Like a dog's love.

My entire world was crumbling again. Was I making the right decision?

To say I was a mess is an understatement. Those were the hardest days of my life. The only light was the brightness of Christmas. I was busy getting everything organized for my family, but at the back of my mind was the thought of soon saying goodbye to my best friend. It still breaks my heart. Euthanasia gives us an opportunity to allow our pets a lovely last day, and so I continued to plan Axel's.

On Boxing Day, all I could think of was the two days until I held his paw and let him go. Logically, I knew what I had to do, but my heart couldn't say goodbye. I should add though, that the one good part is that we 'can say goodbye'. We don't take time for granted but spend every minute cherishing the time we have left with our loved ones before their final day.

Axel spent his last couple of days with me by his side once the children were in bed. On a couple of nights, the week before, we let him into our playroom. As usual, the children were wild, and I could see that it made Axel nervous. He spent most of his time in the front room. This was easier for him, especially as he grew older. It was his safe, quiet place. He had developed anxiety with age. The front entryway was his haven. I can't say I blame him; with three children, I sometimes want a haven too.

The day before I would say goodbye arrived much too quickly. That night, I had a planned to take him for a walk and buy him pizza. Axel spent his last twenty-four hours doing all the things he loved. We went on a hike where he could smell all the smells, just him and me. I took a video of the day and I still watch at times while crying into a pillow. What I would give to walk with him again!

Axel and I had been through everything together! I was distraught. I couldn't stop crying, and the pain was unbearable. In the moment I felt like people would judge me because he was 'just a dog', but he wasn't 'just a dog' to me. He was my best friend and my fur child. He was the one who made me a mom. He was the one who kept me grounded when the ground would slip out from under me. As you can imagine, typing this has me in tears. I have moments where I think I am ok, but then it hits me like a brick wall. What do I do now? He was my crutch in times of stress, he was my support!

I needed to heal and, one night, I wrote him a letter. Yes, I wrote my deceased dog a love letter. I wanted to talk through the regrets. I needed to eliminate the hurt and change it to understanding. When we face loss or struggle, we resort to the negative, intrusive thoughts, the – 'what ifs?' and I 'should-haves'. I wrote about my regrets and how I was sorry but recognized that I couldn't change anything. What I could do was accept being unable to change the past and commit to changing for the future in honour of him. It may seem silly, but it felt great. I read my letter every time panic sets in, and it helps. Writing it was freeing and helped me into the acceptance stage of grief.

Two weeks after his passing, I began to feel truly lost. The week of his passing was incredibly hard until I wrote the letter. I had returned to nursing and had opened a daycare in my home. I felt stressed and was struggling. Axel wasn't there.

I felt as lost as I did at the time we met when my heart had been shattered. Now I had to go on without him. Saying goodbye to Axel was like saying goodbye to one of my children, although he was ready to leave this world.

My book is entitled, "A Dog's Love" because the love a dog gives their human extends beyond anything we have felt or will feel. It binds us to them, it is forever, and it makes us who we are. Axel was a part of me and always will be. We faced so much together. He helped me become a mom and most importantly, he showed me how to love again. I am so grateful for our time together.

All we can do in the most difficult moments is honour the memory of our furry children, and picture them running as they had before across fields with the cows at the farm. Or whatever your pooches loved to do. I imagine Axel in his prime, shaking his bum back and forth as he shook off water from the bath. I remember him wildly tearing around in the yard of our first house. I had forgotten those times; he had slowed as he grew older. He was always loyal and a shoulder to cry on but wasn't happy anymore. There were brief glimpses near the end, but it was never the same. He wanted to run and bum-shake, but he didn't have the energy or coordination anymore. The disease progressed and he faded.

On Axel's last day I didn't leave his side. I organized the children, then spent my time with him. He was having a bad day, and this made it almost easier for me. I took my eldest son with me to the appointment. He was five at the time. But first, we went for a trail walk. Axel loved all the smells. I guess that was the hound in him. As we walked across the high school field back to my car, I felt sick to my stomach. We stopped for a slice of pizza on our way to the clinic. Axel had always loved pizza, and I made sure to give it to him on his last day.

When we arrived at the clinic, I drove around back as asked for privacy-sake. We walked Axel around the parking lot, waiting for the technician and doctor to come out. Axel ate his pizza in the back of my SUV and, of course, sauce was everywhere, but that meant he enjoyed it. When the technician came out, we reviewed the consent form and proceeded with sedation. I knew it would knock Axel off his feet, as he was always sensitive. Within seconds, he was on the ground, and my son had started to panic. It was so hard for both of us, but I wanted him there to understand what was happening and to say goodbye. After all, he was Axel's first baby. After I gave birth to Henry, Axel pretty much became Henry's dog.

I carried Axel into the clinic and laid him on the blanket spread out on the floor of the examination room. He was still with us, but both sedation and disease had weakened him. A catheter was inserted as the doctor came in. My heart beat fast, and tears ran down my face. My son stood frightened in the corner. I may sound like a terrible mother, but I needed Henry. And he needed me. This experience bonded us more closely than ever.

The doctor asked if I was ready, and I nodded in reply. I kept my face close to Axel's and cried again into his fur. I heard his last breaths and knew he was gone before the doctor confirmed. As much as it hurt, there was a calmness in the moment. I still feel he did that for me, letting me know that everything was okay, and that he was ready to pass. I hadn't noticed all his suffering before this day. Maybe I was too busy or in denial. Maybe he put on a brave face knowing I wasn't ready to say goodbye. I had thought that despite my experience, seeing my own dog pass would bring me to my knees, but it didn't. I felt at ease; I cried but I kept my cool.

I confess that through the weeks leading up to, and directly after, my emotions were out of control. However, in that examination room, I was calm, and I thank Axel. In his last moments I felt like our souls merged again and he set me free.

But the calmness faded the moment we returned home. I brought my son into the house then I went outside to gather things from the car, mainly Axel's blanket. As I entered the house and smelled the blanket in my arms, I fell and silently cried out in pain. I didn't want to terrify my kids.

I broke.

Hell, I shattered.

# Chapter 9:
# The Next Chapter

**THE NEXT CHAPTER WAS MESSY.** I felt as I had before Axel had entered my life, lost, swimming in circles. He had been my best friend through it all, and now he was gone. Everyday afterward, the pain hit me like a brick wall, mainly at night. I cried heavily into my pillow thinking about all the regrets. I was in a perpetual cycle of pain, although I knew I made the right decision, a piece of me was missing. We had contemplated getting another dog, but even that weighed me down. I was uneasy about the extra responsibilities a dog would bring but, most of all, I felt anxious because no dog could replace Axel.

Life is full of different chapters and, times in our life, some filled with struggle, while others are welcomed with ease. In the chapter after Axel, I faced more struggles. I hadn't felt as overwhelmed since my first heartbreak and the spiraling events that followed. This was only the beginning of the stresses I faced that year. My family underwent emotional and financial difficulties. Life had taken a turn.

Again, I found my life falling apart and, this time I didn't have Axel. In the early stages of the aftermath, I slowly picked up the pieces, figuring out who I was without him. He had been my security and constant in life, and now, the child in me was terrified. While growing up, I had experienced much change and insecurity, so much so that I found security in every dog that entered my life. Each one had helped me not feel alone and gave me the love I needed. Axel was with me through the struggles in my early adulthood. Without him, I was that scared little girl again, feeling utterly alone. Time passed, and the hole in my heart grew bigger.

One night, drifting off to sleep, I felt comfort and warmth as I began dreaming. I was walking on a trail close to my childhood home. The wind was cool on my face, but the sun shone brightly and warmed my skin. As I drew in a long breath, I gazed across the field adjacent to the trail, taking in the comfort and beauty of the scenery. Off in the distance, I saw Axel barrelling towards me with his tail wagging and I felt whole. The familiarity of his love was soothing. We spent time hugging one another, and he leaned on my legs, almost knocking me over with excitement. I bent down and took in all the love. Time sped by, and I was pulled from the dream. When I woke, my heart fell, but I smiled. I was reminded of his love and the comfort it brought me. In that dream, he pointed me in the direction of our next dog, a breed I never would have chosen.

My husband had always wanted a Great Dane, and so I agreed to at least go and see them.

There we were in a room fill of these gentle giants. And when I say full, I mean full. Picture a small room filled with giant crates and 160-pound dogs. There had to be at least ten and more kept coming in! They were gentle and loving and exactly what I needed. The hole in my heart felt full in that moment. Then the puppies came in, and I melted! It took only five minutes for me to fall in love.

The striking black Great Dane-with fur so sleek, and a distinctive white chest marking that made him stand out, he found my husband first. Then he trotted over to me, and I looked deep into his eyes. There it was, the connection I was looking for! Four weeks later, we brought that handsome-devil home. He was spunky, but terrified when he arrived, it took him nearly a week to adjust but, with three screaming children who could blame. King entered our lives, as Axel had, at a time when our family was struggling. His presence made everything easier. I feel Axel's presence in these moments, together with, the love and memorable times we shared.

A dog's love comes into your life at the time you most need it. The next chapter is a time of healing and growth, a time we sit at peace with our loss and welcome the emotions that come with it. Grief is a tricky emotion, coming in waves and hitting us when we least expect. A dog's love also comes at various stages of life, hitting us when we least expect it.

Eight long months have passed since we said goodbye to Axel. To this moment, I remember that final day and how my heart shattered.

As written earlier, Axel and I used to do a lot of back-country camping together. During those times, his soul was at its freest. Now, Axel's ashes stay in our main living area. Merc often sits with him, nuzzling his urn. He misses his fur brother.

As we planned for our next back-country adventure, my heart felt heavy. After Axel passed, I wanted to spread his ashes on the island he loved and where we had visited while camping. It's also the place where my husband proposed. On our last camping trip, I was six months pregnant with our first-born son who turns six this year.

The day came and we were ready to head into the wilderness for Axel's last adventure. His ashes were the last thing to be packed. My heart couldn't bear to spread them all, and I put half into a Ziploc bag. I stood on our front porch holding his cedar urn with "Axel" etched into the top. I opened the navy-blue silk bag and reached in. Maybe I should have spread them in their entirety, but my heart couldn't let go.

Our eight-month-old Great Dane puppy, two toddlers, and two adults all packed into the VW Tiguan. Our eldest was already at his grandparent's house. The morning before we left, we had awakened with eagerness, it was going to be a kid free weekend, other than for King. My husband had packed our gear and food the night before, tucking Axel safely into the dry bag in case we headed overboard. This was King's first canoe camping trip. We weren't sure how he would feel about it. But the long trek into, and out of, the park was a success. We all stayed dry!

The morning was misty and foggy. As we paddled across the first lake, the fog left a chill in the air. It was a long trek into the park. First, a long paddle across a lake and into a ravine of swampy water, followed by two portages. Overall, it was windy and not a good day. We found a site and settled in. The weather left us with an eerie feeling. Our campsite was across from the island where we would lay Axel to rest. When we arrived, the island campsite we had frequented had been occupied and so, we found our own little island and the best campsite, across the way. There was only us, and King loved it. It had a pleasant beach with a rock-face and fire-pit, a campsite we will certainly return to.

After settling in, we scavenged for firewood and set up for the night. The next day was cleared, and we were able to enjoy the trip more. From where we were, we saw that the people staying on the big island had left, and we made our way across with Axel. We scoped out the site and laid him to rest by a tree with small rocks spelling his name. The area was removed from activity. I unzipped his ashes and dumped them. It wasn't very graceful, but Axel never was, and neither am I. As I let go, I thought of everything we had gone through, the good and the bad; all those moments we spent on the island. Emotions ran over me, but it felt liberating. I pictured Axel running back and forth between the trees and two campsites. I saw him sunbathing and hiding in the bushes when things were too much for him. Most of all, I felt him leaning on me and nuzzling his snout into my legs.

King was with us, and I am not sure he understood what we were doing, but he picked up on the emotions. I kept my composure; I knew Axel would be free there. I even talked to him as though he was still alive.

That night, we took a paddle around the small island to see the tree. I spoke to him again. It was an emotional moment, but I felt more at peace, and having King there helped. He was wonderful throughout the trip, aside from eating our sponge on day one. He still hasn't passed it, but I am hoping for the best. A dog's love distracts us, remember?

It has been a week since we left the site, and I've been trying to settle into work and life again. Life in the woods is peaceful and quiet whereas the usual daily chaos can be overwhelming. It has taken me this long since we've been moving so fast from one thing to the next. I haven't had time to process and needed to deal with it all, so here I am.

The trip was a success. Not only did it bond us with King, but it helped my marriage and our connection. Part of me believes that was

Axel's doing. Even after returning home, I feel Axel and the familiar connection. During the camping trip, I watched King tearing around the campsite with his bum tucked in, something Axel often did.

Since coming home, I see more in King that reminds me of Axel, as if the weekend in the woods awoke something in King. I'm a spiritual person and believe that when we leave this earth, we always return.

I believe that with King, Axel did find his way back to me.

And just at the right time.

# Chapter 10:
# A Dog's Love

**A DOG'S LOVE UNTANGLES THE KNOT** in our stomachs. You know the knot I'm talking about, the one that makes us sick with worry. For me, a dog's love helped deal with feeling alone as a child. Each dog that entered my life gave me unconditional love, the one thing I longed for. I yearned for security, to feel safe and be myself. This is something I've come to see only as an adult. My parents were loving and gave me a sound upbringing, but I felt too sheltered, almost like I was hiding. Being seen as weak would disappoint them, so I hid my emotions. Through the years, I developed the coping skill of avoidance and faced my emotions alone; that is until "a dog's love" – entered my life.

Such love alleviates pain and helps us see a piece of ourselves. Each dog that came into my life helped me see that it was fine to have feelings and emotions and be myself. I received their love without condition.

The same reigns true today. With each struggle I encounter, I'm comforted by a dog's love. Last year, that love was shared with Axel in his last months. His disease progressed, but he held strong for me, and I tried to be strong for him. Today, I'm with King in times of struggle. His presence helps me again feel the connection I had with Axel. He helps soothe me after a bad day or when I feel lonely. His bouncy self helps me cope with the everyday chaos that is my life. As my children do, he finds ways to make me laugh, alleviating tension reminding me to be free in the moments and take it all in.

A dog's love is a reminder that time is fleeting, and their furry, loving presence shows us that every day is a blessing. Those who have found a dog's love, know how special it is. Those who have yet to find that soul connection, know that it will happen at a time you need it most.

To heal you.

To help you grow.

To live with you always.

For those who have lost their furry best friend, hold on, better days are ahead.

Your furry loved one isn't far from you. They are always by your side, sitting, waiting, and wagging until the next time you meet.

# A Brief Thank You

I'M TAKING THIS OPPORTUNITY TO THANK you for reading my book to the end. The loss of furry family members can be devastating, and I wanted you to know you are never alone. They're always with you, even after crossing the Rainbow Bridge. The book is about the special bond that dog's have with us. I've never been someone who immediately connects with other people but bring me a dog, and I can feel their souls. Dogs are special beings. Each one that entered my life has left a paw print on my heart.

Axel was the one that helped me grow and heal.

King is the one that helped me find myself again.

Each dog's love serves a purpose.

For those who may still wonder about the sponge, King finally vomited it up. How it sat in his stomach for two weeks, I'll never know!

# Letter to Axel

Dear Axel,

You were the most amazing dog.

Although you tested my patience, and won on more then one occasion, you were the best thing that ever happened to me. When you came into my life, I was a mess. I didn't know what I wanted, or where I wanted to be. You changed that with your patience and your love, which helped me heal and rebuild myself.

My heart had been shattered when we met, but you worked to repair it, no questions asked. You listened, nuzzled, and loved unconditionally. You tested me, and I sometimes failed; for that I am sorry. I regret not spending as much time with you as I should have after having my children. It didn't mean I didn't love you but only that I was tired and busy. I saw how they overwhelmed you and that you needed to rest too. That never meant you loved them any less. In fact, you embraced being a big brother, and I'm eternally grateful for that. You were their first dog just as you were mine.

You left paw-prints on our hearts. There's so much I want to share but you already know. I can feel your gentle nudge telling me it's okay. I still hear your bed squeaking, your ears flapping when you shake, and your toes clicking on the floor. I miss your smell, the good and the bad. I miss you. Every minute of every day. There are times I think I'm okay, but then other times when I break down while cleaning the cat litter, remembering how you liked to do that with me.

There are so many memories, and I don't want to avoid them. I want to always remember you and I vow to keep you in my children's memories as well. You were the most amazing dog, Axman, aka Stinky Pants. I can never let you go. I know you were ready to say goodbye and that I held on too long. I see now in your photos that you were ready for a long time. I remember you as a young boy full of spunk. I remember you wiggling your bum and your "mood ear" that always kinked when you were happy. You had good moments like these near the end, and they were wonderful to see, but you were sad for most of the time. I'm glad I could give you the peaceful passing you deserved. You've been through so much, Axman, both before and with me. I hope I made your life exactly what you wanted. My love for you goes beyond this world.

You were my first love and my rock after my first real heartbreak. As I say goodbye, know that I'll be okay because you taught me how. You paved the way for me to become a mom and helped me transition into the role with my human babies. You've given me so much, Axel, over these past fourteen years. Thank you, a million times over. I love you so much, and I accept that there are things I cannot change. Regrets that I can only learn from, and I especially will learn to make time every day to take in every moment. In the last part of your life, you helped me transition by making your passage over the Rainbow Bridge so smooth. I wondered why I felt so calm when I only wanted to scream in pain. You were telling me that you were ready, and I'm at peace with that. I accept that I wasn't always there for you and that I can't change the past. I accept that it's alright to be happy, even though you're not here, by honouring you best I can. I can honour you by staying true to these words.

May you run with Rueger and eat all the pizza you want! I know that Nanny is up there with you; she loved you! You were what she needed at the time she met you with her Alzheimer's Disease. You made her smile, and I know she's squeezing you right now!

I love you always and forever, sweet boy.
Lots of kisses.
Merc sends his love too.
Mom xoxo

# About the Author

**AS A CHILD OF DIVORCE,** I had a lot of uncertainty and change in my life growing up. As each dog love entered my life, with them they brought comfort and security.

I am a mom of three beautiful children and have been married for eight years. I work in the community as a nurse, as well as at the local hospital. I decided to write this book shortly after saying goodbye to my dog of fourteen years. He was my everything. We met at a time in my life where I was struggling. I was working as a Veterinary Technician, single and living on my own. His love was exactly what I needed in that time of my life. Unknown to me when we met, we had more in common then I thought.

Writing has always been a passion of mine, but one I gave up shortly after high school. After having children, I have begun to dive back into it as a way to hold emotions and cope. I hold power in the words I place on a page, and bring comfort to those who read them.

I spent eight years as a Veterinary Technician before deciding to change careers. I have witnessed and felt the impact a dog's love provides to their owner. I have seen and felt first hand how important their existence in our lives truly is. I wrote this book to honor this bond and this love. May you find comfort in my words.

Peg, knowing you has been
such an amazing journey.
From the stories you tell, you've
lived such an amazing life.
In this last day, may the goddess
bring you home + embrace you
with pure love + harmony.

Thank you for being such an
amazing person + allowing me
to be part of the journey.

your dogs are waiting for you

♡

A dog's love always waits.

*(signature)*

CPSIA information can be obtained
at www.ICGtesting.com
Printed in the USA
LVHW040224240623
750321LV00002B/104

9 781039 175501